W9-CSZ-280

Feeding the World

Janine Amos

RSVP

RAINTREE
STECK-VAUGHN
PUBLISHERS
The Steck-Vaughn Company
Austin, Texas

Editor: A. Patricia Sechi
Designer: Shaun Barlow
Project Manager: Joyce Spicer
Electronic Production: Scott Melcer
Artwork: David Farren
Cover Artwork: David Farren
Picture Research: Ambreen Husain
Educational Advisor: Joy Richardson

Library of Congress
Cataloging-in-Publication Data
Amos, Janine.
    Feeding the world /
Janine Amos.
        p.   cm. — (First starts)
    Includes index.
    Summary: Examines the problem of hunger in developing countries and discusses possible solutions.
    Hardcover   ISBN 0-8114-3407-9
    Softcover   ISBN 0-8114-4918-1
    1. Food supply — Juvenile literature. 2. Poor — Juvenile literature. 3. Malnutrition — Juvenile literature. 4. Food supply — Developing countries — Juvenile literature. 5. Poor — Developing countries — Juvenile literature. 6. Malnutrition — Developing countries — Juvenile literature. [1. Food supply. 2. Poor. 3. Malnutrition.]   I. Title.   II. Series.
HD9000.5.A543 1993
338.1'9—dc20   92-16337
                            CIP AC
Printed and bound in the United States by Lake Book, Melrose Park, IL

2 3 4 5 6 7 8 9 0 LB 98 97 96 95 94 93

Contents

Why Is Food Important?

Everyone needs food. We need it to keep us alive. We need food to keep us healthy, to give us energy, and to help us grow. But in some parts of the world many people do not have enough to eat. They spend their whole lives suffering from **hunger**.

▽ Food gives us energy to work and play.

Food for Health

It hurts to be hungry. Hungry people can **starve**, or die from lack of food. To be healthy we need a mixture of different foods, or we become weak and ill. More than 600 million people do not have the foods to stay healthy. Most of these people live in the world's poor countries.

▷ These children are able to eat healthy fruits.

◁ △ We need
some of all these
foods to keep us
healthy.

5

Rich Lands

The world's rich or **industrial lands** can feed themselves. Farms are large, and farmers use modern machines. The mild weather is good for many **crops**.

There is usually plenty of food, and if some food is left over, it is stored or sold. If there is not enough food, rich countries can buy it from other countries.

▷ Stores in industrial countries sell foods from many lands.

▽ Farmers use electric motors to run milking machines.

▽ Farmers in rich countries use combine harvesters to help them farm.

▽ Huge greenhouses
keep crops at just the
right temperature.

Poor Lands

Other areas of the world struggle to feed themselves. Some of these are called **developing countries.** There is little industry. Most people work on the land. They farm small plots of ground.

Families are large because these people need children to help them in the fields.

▽ This farmer in the Himalayas uses the same tools as his grandfather did.

▷ Some families work in other villages at harvest time. They are "paid" in food.

▽ Many people in developing countries cannot buy the food they need. They grow much of what they eat.

9

Too Wet, Too Dry

Many developing countries do not grow enough food. Some of these lands have heavy rains that wash away soil and crops. Insects may eat the crops and cause disease. Sometimes it may not rain for months. Then the soil dries up and the crops wither and die. Farm animals die, too.

▷ Clouds of insects called locusts can eat fields of crops in a few hours.

▽ Plants need water to grow. A **drought** has killed this corn crop.

△ Too much rain
can cause a flood.
Whole fields of rice
are destroyed.

Using the Land

In many developing countries good farmland is used for growing **cash crops** like sugar and coffee. These crops are not used for food by the local people. They are sold to other countries. Each year there is less land for growing food, but more people to feed. The soil is overused so crops do not grow well.

▽ Too many goats on this land are destroying the soil.

▽ Many African farmers grow only cash crops like cotton.

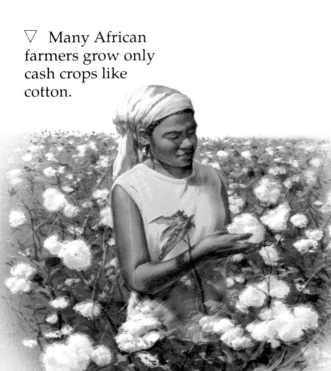

▽ Sugarcane grows well in hot, wet countries.

▽ Overusing the land turns it into desert.

War

In wartime people may go hungry. Families may leave their homes quickly to find safety. They often leave with no food, and their crops are left to rot in the fields. In wartime soldiers may destroy food crops or stop food from being delivered.

▷ In 1991 war forced many Kurdish people to live in **refugee** camps.

◁ In some countries farmland is destroyed by fighting. Farmers are driven away and people go hungry.

Emergency

Disasters like floods, drought, or war can leave people starving. Millions of people may die from lack of food. This news quickly reaches other countries. Charities and **government** leaders decide how much help, or **aid**, to send. Charities and famous people also collect money. It will be used to send food to the hungry.

▷ A music concert called Live Aid was a special event held to help people in Africa.

▽ In 1991 huge winds and waves ruined crops in Bangladesh. Millions were left homeless and hungry.

▽ Television
brings us news of
an emergency in a
developing country.

Food Aid

Food sent to people in need is called **food aid**. In an emergency, food must arrive quickly. It is taken to the country by ship or airplane. Then trucks or helicopters carry the food to special centers. Here people gather to be fed. For some people it arrives too late.

△ It takes time and money to get food aid to the people who need it.

▷ In a war delivering food aid can be dangerous. When there is fighting, food may be brought by helicopter.

Food for Life

Food aid is often grain like corn, rice, wheat, and millet. In an emergency this food saves lives. But millions of tons of food are sent to developing countries every year. Local farmers still grow these crops, but they also grow new ones.

▽ This child is too ill to eat. But a mixture of sugar, salt, and water will keep her alive.

△ Clean drinking water is important. In an emergency it may be brought to an area in a truck.

△ A meal for each person will be just one handful of this wheat.

△ Milk is a food that is given to help the hungry. It comes as powder to which water is added.

Working Together

Developing countries need to be able to feed themselves. To do this the farmers must be able to make their land produce more crops. Projects are being set up to try out better farming methods. Other countries are helping by sending money, machinery, and people to work with local farmers.

▷ Farmers in Ethiopia dig terraces to keep the water from running down the hillsides.

▽ Villagers learn to build little stone or earth walls called diguettes. They trap rainwater to help crops grow.

▷ Handpumps bring water to dry villages. Villagers learn how to take care of the pump.

▷ Farmers in hot
lands learn to keep
the soil damp with
mounds of earth.

Helping Themselves

Workers from other countries work with villagers. The workers teach families about food and health. Families may make small vegetable gardens or learn to keep chickens. In some villages, health centers are set up.

▽ At this center, families are having lessons on food and health.

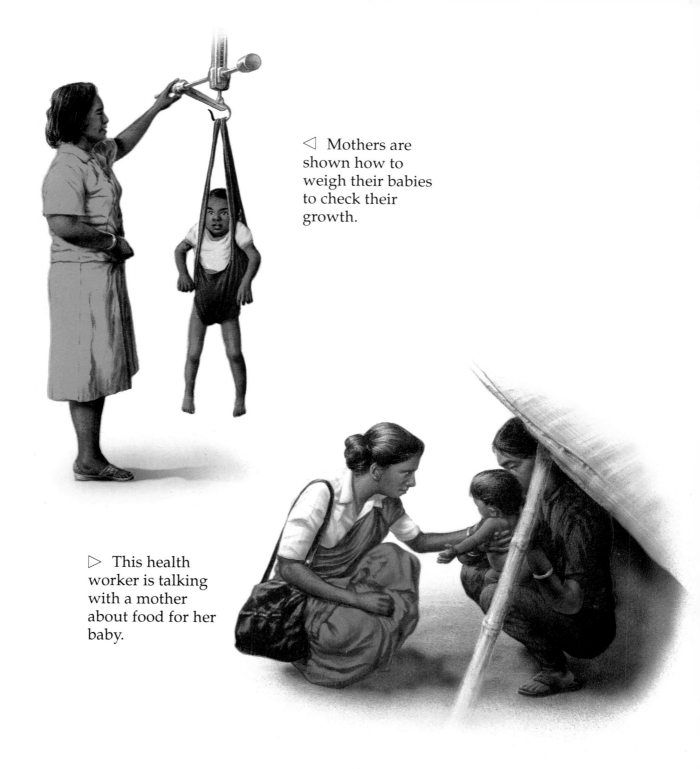

◁ Mothers are shown how to weigh their babies to check their growth.

▷ This health worker is talking with a mother about food for her baby.

Food and Science

Scientists are working on the world's food problem. They are trying to make new kinds of grain that will grow quickly without harmful or expensive fertilizers. They are trying to make new and tasty foods from plants that grow well in hot countries. Experts are studying insect pests and how to control them.

▷ Fast-growing seeds give several harvests from the same plot of land each year.

▽ Soybeans, nuts, and coconuts may be important foods for the future.

▽ Scientists are learning about the diseases that kill crops.

△ This expert is helping a farmer get rid of insects in his cabbage crop.

Success Stories

People in poor countries can feed themselves if they are given the chance. Money from the government in Zimbabwe helped small farmers to grow corn. Villagers in Tanzania increased their milk supply with the help of overseas workers. And children in Mali learned how to grow vegetables for the school cafeteria.

▷ This boy is gathering food he has grown on his new land.

▽ Zimbabwe's small farmers have become big corn farmers.

▽ The people of Saba Island now earn a living from the sea. They grow seaweed for sale.

▷ These cows were dying from insect bites. Overseas aid helped villagers to build a cattle dip to protect the cows.

Things to Do

Feeding the world is a problem, and there is a lot of work to be done. We can all help. You can help by:

• Buying gifts and other foods from stores that help small businesses in developing countries.

• Collecting money for charities like Oxfam and UNICEF. Could your school do something to raise money? Ask your family and friends to write to one of these organizations:

Useful Addresses:

Bread for the World
802 Rhode Island Avenue, NE
Washington, DC 20018

CARE
660 First Avenue
New York, NY 10016

Oxfam America
115 Broadway
Boston, MA 02116

UNICEF Headquarters
UNICEF House
3 United Nation Plaza
New York, NY 10017

Glossary

aid Help given to a country or people.

cash crop A crop such as sugar, rice, cotton, or coffee that is grown for sale to other countries.

crop A plant grown for people to use.

developing country A country with few industries, where most of the people earn a living from the land. Africa, India, and parts of South America are developing countries.

drought A long period of very dry weather.

food aid Help in the form of food.

government The leaders of a country.

hunger Serious need for food. Weakness from lack of food. A serious food shortage in an area is called a famine.

industrial lands Countries where most people earn a living by producing goods.

refugee A person forced to leave his or her home, usually in a time of war.

starve To die of hunger or suffer very badly from lack of food.

Index

Photographic credits: Heather Angel cover, 27; Biofotos 10; Ecoscene 5; Mark Edwards/Still Pictures cover, 13, 20; Hutchison Library 3, 7, 24; Oxfam 23; Panos Pictures 8, 15, 19, 29; Frank Spooner Pictures 17.